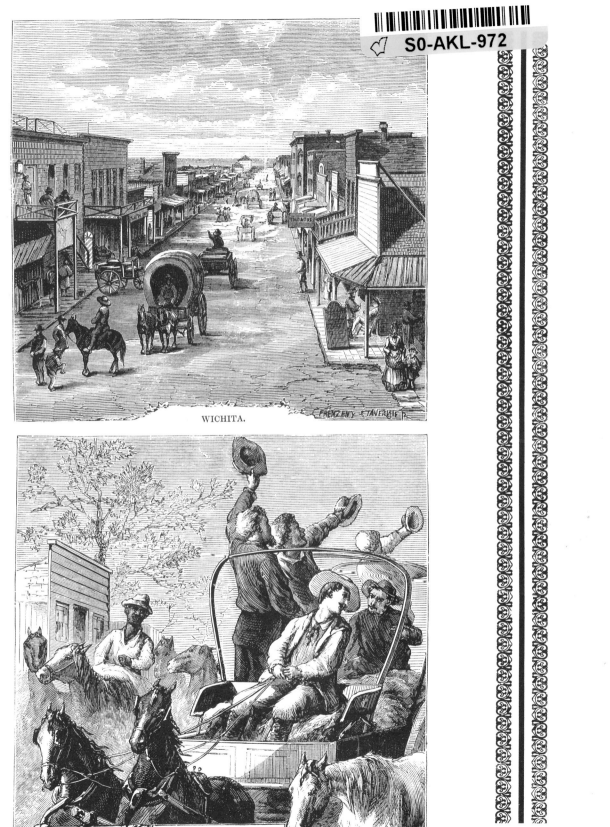

WICHITA.

HO, FOR TEXAS!

THE COWBOY

in
American
Prints

Also edited by John Meigs

Peter Hurd, The Lithographs
Peter Hurd Sketch Book

THE COWBOY in American Prints

edited by JOHN MEIGS

SAGE BOOKS

THE SWALLOW PRESS INC.
CHICAGO

Sage Books are published by
The Swallow Press Incorporated
1139 South Wabash Avenue
Chicago, Illinois 60605

ISBN 0-8040-0597-4
Library of Congress Catalog Card
Number 72-88595

The first printing consists of five
thousand copies, of which three hundred
are signed and numbered and include
an original lithograph done especially
for this book by Peter Hurd, and twenty-
six (not for sale) signed and lettered
and include the special Hurd lithograph.

To Henriette and Peter who have so generously shared their love of this beautiful land

CONTENTS

Illus. 1

INTRODUCTION

The American Cowboy—over a hundred years have not dimmed his image or diffused his spirit. In his original version he was a pared down, lean, practical man with no excess in person or paraphernalia. He followed the time-honored profession of herding cattle, but he put his own individual stamp on the job as no other had done before. He loved hard, played hard, fought elements and other men when the occasion arose. He had a job that could not be called glamorous or good paying or desirable, and it was equipped with built-in danger and pain and death. It is difficult to conceive how he became the most American of American images, over-shadowing the Paul Bunyans and the Davy Crocketts and more swiftly fading symbols. The American Cowboy has been psychoanalyzed and emulated. He has been both falsely represented and genuinely portrayed in books and movies. Often he has written his own story, yet others have shaped his image to their various ends. He rises again and again, recreated by each generation in its own likeness; he is all the good and brave and idealistic images we wish to make of him.

But where did all this begin? How did this unlikely figure, lost in a faraway stretch of the West, unknown in person or by personal deed, emerge as such a potent American symbol? He was, in part, created by an army of artists, writers, and illustrators.

The middle of the 19th century, caught up in the midst of the industrial revolution, created a desire for knowledge on all levels, and the periodicals of the last half of the century set about the business of providing knowledge, information, and adventure for the masses. They were ably aided by new and speedier processes of printing and illustrating, and this called for journalists and artists who could spread out across the land and record every facet of a vast and growing country.

Illus. 2

The cowboy was discovered and his hard existence glamorized by the pen and pencil of these writer-explorers. (The word "cowboy," however, was twenty years or more away from these journalistic beginnings, and in spite of many claims no one has offered a fool-proof explanation of the coining of the word. It was originally hyphenated "cow-boy" and was so spelled into the 1880s.) They usually revealed his actual contours, yet were not above certain fabrications, and those confined to their desks in the east evolved the most imaginative images of all.

Profusely illustrated American periodicals began in the 1850s and proliferated rapidly. *Harper's Weekly Illustrated Magazine* was the front runner. *Gleason's Pictorial* was another early starter; in the June 26 issue of 1852 they ran a front-page illustration of rounding up wild horses in Texas (Illus. 1), possibly the first depiction. Other publications followed, such as *The Century Illustrated Monthly Magazine, Frank Leslie's Illustrated Weekly, Scribner's Monthly,* and *Police Gazette.* All sent out a growing group of reporters and authors to search out adventure in the west, a west extensively explored by an earlier generation, but exciting nonetheless.

The public loved it and avidly read the accounts of life on ranches and the daring-do of manly types who fought Indians with one hand and roped cows with the other. The cowboy was early given a hell-raising character as part of his image; certainly he earned the privilege, for his often lonely existence and the long journeys to the rail head where the cattle were shipped entitled him to celebrations of more than modest proportions. The Texas cowboy, presumably the first on the scene or certainly the first to emerge as a special type, was particularly noted for his excesses, and accounts in local newspapers gave him ample play when he went on a rampage and shot up the local saloon or, on occasion, the whole town and some of the local citizenry. Prowling reporters picked up many of these tales for the readers back home and often were witnesses to actual events which they recounted in blood-red detail.

The earliest artists, however, were content to portray the milder aspects of life on the prairie. For example, the illustrations in McCoy's *Historic Sketches of the Cattle Trade in the West and Southwest* depicted mainly the everyday jobs of the cowboy: working cattle, rounding up, marking and branding, cattle driving; but one drawing also showed them kicking up their heels to the sprightly music of fiddle and bass (Illus. 4). Ladies were few and far between in the ranch areas and it is presumed that those shown were at some frontier town of the period and were of "easy virtue"—to judge by the generous display of leg.

In 1866 Theodore R. Davis and Alfred R. Waud, who began as field illustrators for *Harper's Weekly* during the Civil War, went west on assignment from the editors of *Harper's;*

Illus. 3

from this venture came some of the earliest portrayals of the cowboy and his life. Waud created what is probably the first depiction in print from life of actual cowboy activity. Entitled "A Drove of Texas Cattle Crossing a Stream," it appeared in the October 19 issue of *Harper's Weekly* in 1867 (Plate 1).

Many illustrators also wrote about their experiences. Waud probably penned this description which appeared with his 1867 rendering: "A drove of 500 cattle is usually accompanied by a dozen men, drivers, cook, etc. mounted upon mustang pon-

ies, a wild set, who plunge in and out of rivers, or rush among stampeders in the most reckless ways."

William M. Cary, who had gone west as an illustrator in 1861, made a second trip in 1874; his "Cattle Raid on the Texas Border" (Plate 2) shows vaqueros and cowboys in a wild shooting melee, with cattle and sheep herded together in what was to become in later history of the west an impossible mixture.

About this time *Harper's,* still in the forefront with its widely read publication, sent west a team of French artists, Paul Frenzeny and Jules Tavernier. Both had backgrounds of military experience, Frenzeny in France and Mexico and Tavernier in the Franco-Prussian War, which provided them with the horsemanship necessary for their western jaunts. They had worked as a team before and continued to do so in the west. Robert Taft, in his excellent book, *Artists and Illustrators of*

Illus. 5

Illus. 6

the Old West, says, "The division of labor in this partnership can only be guessed at. Comparison of the sketches by the individuals with those bearing the joint signatures is of little aid, as the wood engraver reduced nearly all illustrations to the same level." In this present volume the rear endpaper, "Taming and Training the American Mustang," represents drawings by Frenzeny alone. Illustrations 2, 5, and 6, Plates 3 and 4, and the front endpaper, "The Texas Cattle Trade," are examples of joint work by Frenzeny and Tavernier. Illustration 6, "On the Trail," reflects how even fine artists sometimes relied too heavily on imgination or writers' descriptions; this cattle drive, with its neat and orderly line, was a far cry from the actual milling herd on the trail.

In 1875 a *Harper's* illustration by W. J. Palmer, "Driving Cattle into a Corral in the Far West" (Plate 5), gave the feeling of an actual incident, although some of the cowboys pictured

5

Illus. 7

Illus. 8

appear to be Indians.

The Civil War had been over for ten years at this time and many of the more adventurous spirits from both armies had found life at home extremely dull after the excitement and comradery of war. The west, while settled on the edges, still presented an enticing prospect; and with little thought to what means of livelihood they might apprentice themselves, they went west.

Joseph Nimmo, writing in *Harper's* in the 1880s, claimed that the beginning of the great catte industry could be traced

Illus. 9

to an incident that befell a government trader in 1864. Early in December of that year on his way to Camp Douglas in the Territory of Utah, he was overtaken on the Laramie Plains by an unusually severe snowstorm. He was compelled to go into winter quarters at once. He turned his cattle loose, expecting they would soon perish from exposure and starvation. They remained about the camp and as the snow was blown off the highlands the dried grass afforded them an abundance of food. When spring arrived they were found to be in even better condition than when they were turned out. This led to an experi-

ment of herding cattle in the northern ranges, but for years it was a slow and hazardous business. Depredations by "Reservation Indians" who were allowed to forage for food in the summer also caused great losses; the cattle were easier game than the almost-gone buffalo, and in their sport, according to Nimmo, they occasionally lifted the scalp of a stray cowboy.

In Texas the cattle trade had long since been established and herds were driven west to the army posts located throughout the southwest and to the Mississippi where they were shipped by boat to eastern markets. The railroads were beginning to

Illus. 11

Illus. 12

Illus. 13

edge west at this time, along with the telegraph wires, and William F. Sparks in 1881 pictured "cattle herders" (note the term) indulging in revolver practice at telegraph insulators (Illus. 7). L. W. MacDonald depicted scenes around Kerrville, Texas for *Leslie's Weekly* (Illus. 9), including a stampede of thunder-frightened cattle (Plate 8), an event which must have seemed high adventure to ex-soldiers and would-be cowboys in the east. When they arrived "out west," however, they found that "adventure" meant hard work, discomfort, and a high incidence of lead poisoning.

Of all the early illustrators who came west to work for the periodicals, W. A. Rogers must rank with the finest early artists of actual cowboy life. An illustrator for *Harper's* as early as 1877, he made an exciting trip to the northern territory and

Canada in 1878. When he was assigned by *Harper's* great editor, Charles Parsons, to investigate the southwest with the magazine's writer, A. A. Hayes, he was ready and eager to return westward. A sojourn in Colorado led to a trip by the pair to a ranch belonging to "Uncle" Pete Dotson. While Hayes wrote about the profits that could be made in ranching, Rogers had his first opportunity to depict cowboys from life. Though his cattle were none too good, his earlier drawing experience as a cartoonist for the *Daily Graphic* in New York stood him in good stead and his characters in "Betting on the Bull-fight" (Plate 6) and "Breaking Camp" (Plate 7) are particularly human and natural. The work is quite a departure from previously engraved pictures in periodicals and laid a foundation for the style of engraving which gave Frederic Remington's work such vigor and authenticity.

This western trip provided two other illustrations in 1882 and 1883 respectively, "Life in a Dug-out" (Plate 10) and "Lassoing and Branding Calves" (Plate 11). Rogers, incidentally, portrayed small boys in two of these engravings, but no ladies are included; however, one can feel the beginning of the civilizing influence of women in the background.

The notes accompanying Rogers' illustrations used the term "cow-boy" and stated that "The cow-boys of the Rocky Mountain regions are a race or a class peculiar to that country. They have some resemblance to the corresponding class on the southern side of the Rio Grande, but are of a milder and more original type."

It was no doubt due to his western experience that he was called upon to redraw "a Sketch by Frederic Remington"—

"Roused by a Scout" (Plate 9)—which had been submitted by the young artist after a trip west. Rogers made several more western visits in his long career as an illustrator, but apparently he did not return to the cowboy as subject matter.

The cattle country came in for more and more interest as the illustrators spread out across the west. Ranches were depicted by this time as organized, permanent establishments such as those shown in Illustrations 10 and 11. "Home on a Cattle Ranch" (San Miguel County, New Mexico) and "Herding Cattle in New Mexico" showed that other areas besides Texas and Colorado were settling down to the profitable side of ranching. The railroad, by now an established fixture running through the center of the country, was the means of getting the cattle to the eastern markets which were rapidly replacing the army forts and outposts as outlets for the burgeoning industry. And industry it now was.

Rufus F. Zogbaum was a noted illustrator of military life and in his trips west to give graphic dimension to army life he fell in with the spell of the vast country and its people. From a trip to Montana in the mid-1880s and a later trip to Oklahoma Territory in 1888, he gathered material which was responsible for a subject copied by many artists in later times, the cowboy at play. His portrayal of "Painting the Town Red" (Plate 12) shows a group of cowboys riding hell-bent-for-leather into a small town, frightening horses and an unfortunate Chinaman, but generally received with amusement by the townspeople and with a hearty cheer by a couple of fellow cowboys already in their cups. His cowboy illustrations added to the increasing interest that was building the cowboy myth among the American

COLLIER'S

VOL. TWENTY-SEVEN NO 24   NEW YORK SEPTEMBER 14 1901   PRICE TEN CENTS

No more he rides, yon waif
    of might;
  His was the song the eagle
    sings;
Strong as the eagle's his de-
    light,
  For like his rope, his heart
    had wings.
        —OWEN WISTER.

Illus. 16

populace. It was also the beginning of the real boom in cowboy illustrations; Remington was just over the horizon with his greatest of all contributions to the image of the cowboy.

William M. Thayer in his 1887 book *Marvels of the New West* described the life of the cowboy in glowing terms while an anonymous artist showed cowboys pulling a cow from a mud hole (Illus. 12) and a cowboy picking up a coin on the ground from the back of a racing horse (Illus. 13). At last the public was getting a more complete picture of what was going on out there in the cattle country. While the hell-raising cowboy was still there he had been endowed with special virtues and a slight halo of respectability by his recorders. The image was about to be furthered by the writers and artists who would be called upon to furnish more and more romantic fodder for the growing number of periodicals and publishing houses.

12

Illus. 17

Illus. 18

Illus. 19

Frederic C. Remington was the right talent at the right time. Railroads brought stabilization to the western plains and the army's ruthless control of the "Indian problem" started a whole new movement west, composed of all classes including immigrants and a few "gentlemen" of standing. Among these were Owen Wister, Theodore Roosevelt, Emerson Hough, and Frederic Remington. Fortunately for the west and the cowboy myth, they could write about and illustrate what they saw, and what they saw was a new land, full of vigor, healthful outdoor living, and the rewards of industry ready for the taking.

The first three wrote about it for the next two decades and Remington was to illustrate it for another twenty years. Beginning with his illustration of Arizona cowboys in 1882, redrawn by W. A. Rogers (Plate 9), he followed up in 1887 with a *Harper's* rendering of the cowboy at play, if such it could be

14   Illus. 20

called, in "A Quarrel Over Cards" (Plate 13). Remington had come west as early as 1881 after a year and a half at Yale Art School. An inheritance from his father, who died in 1880, gave him the funds for the trip and provided him with the money to buy a "ranch" in south-central Kansas. Consisting of only 160 acres, his "ranch" was actually a small area for sheep, but such was the then-prevailing Kansas idea about the most practical way to utilize small plots economically. Cowboys coming from bigger ranch country to the west to cattle towns like Newton, Kansas and Dodge City had created a mystique that the new eastern ranchers were anxious to emulate. So they dressed and talked like their western counterparts, believing themselves to be ranchers in the full sense. Remington fell in at once with the spirit of the group around him, many of whom were bachelors in search of adventure and, hopefully, a livelihood. About a year and a half after he purchased his "ranch" in Kansas, a series of events, including a growing realization that he was not cut out to be a rancher, resulted in the sale of his property and the return to his real love, illustrating and painting. By 1888 he began the great period of his cowboy illustration for *Century Magazine* in a series of drawings for articles by Theodore Roosevelt on ranch life in the west. With such titles as "Ranch Life in the Far West," "The Home Ranch," "Sheriff's Work on a Ranch," and "Ranchman's Rifle on Crag and Prairie," the

15

Illus. 22   Illus. 23

young Remington came into his full stride. In such splendid depiction as "The Herd at Night" (Illus. 14) he was beginning the work that a dozen years later would culminate in his galloping cowboy on the cover of *Collier's,* September 14, 1901 (Illus. 15) accompanied by a poem of the then-famous Owen Wister, author of *The Virginian* and a rancher in Dakota.

Taking themes which were basic and natural to real ranch life such as a bucking bronco (Illus. 17), roping cows (Illus. 19) and cowboys at play (Illus. 18), Remington achieved unsurpassed realism which would be emulated for decades to come. He did a series on the cowboys of Texas, Arizona, and Montana with great authority (Illus. 21) and he showed life

as it actually was: saddling broncs (Illus. 20) and stringing a rope corral for the horses (Illus. 16). He drew horses and men that were one homogeneous animal. His cowboys rode with assurance and ease in performing their myriad duties of breaking horses, roping, and trailing cattle (Illus. 22, 23, 24).

As an accompaniment for Remington's illustration, the text of Theodore Roosevelt's articles was laden with vivid accounts of the "good life" of the rancher as well as the adventures and occasional dangers of such an existence. Roosevelt had gone to the Dakotas in 1883 and purchased a ranch there which was to be the basis for much of his later writing about the west and ranching. He spoke with enthusiasm, and America listened.

16

Illus. 24 *Illus. 25*

Remington used all his ingenuity and talent in drawing the varied and fascinating tales of the west that Roosevelt unfolded. "A Row in a Cattle Town" (Illus. 26) was full of violence. The perils of the herd (Illus. 27) and the dangers of nature (Illus. 28, 29) were graphically portrayed. The illustrations in *Century* were small because of the page size, but they managed to convey much. "An Episode in the Opening Up of a Cattle Country" (Plate 14) is filled with the detail which Remington loved to display and his large collection of actual costumes and artifacts was used to good advantage in his eastern studio where he eventually settled. In 1906 he strongly and publicly criticized Charles Schreyvogel's "Custer's Demand," claiming a lack of authenticity in costume and equipment. In "The Round-up" (Plate 15) he showed a great sensitivity to landscape, which he was to return to in his later paintings. It was a repeat of the tranquil atmosphere created in "The Herd at Night" of the same year. All in all, in a year's time, he had given flesh to the image of the cowboy and his life as no other artist up to that time had even attempted. His success can be measured by the increasing demand for more information and stories of the cowboy life, so that a whole group of writers and illustrators rose to the occasion, only partially as capable as Roosevelt and Remington.

At this time, R. Chapin illustrated *Ten Years a Cowboy,*

17

Illus. 26

anonymously published in 1888; his illustration, "A Happy Ranche" (Illus. 39), shows a dugout with a well-stocked larder of deer carcasses hanging from the eaves. Other illustrators contributed different styles; some pictures of various ranches resemble plates from the popular county histories of the period (for a price you could have your ranch and its improvements depicted in a naive and wooden style). Other books of the period included Emerson Hough's *The Story of the Cowboy*, illustrated by William L. Wells. Wells owed a portion of his style to

H. W. Hansen, who did not spend much time in illustration, but achieved a special distinction in painting the west and its romantic images in oils; although he visited the southwest for details and stories, Wells produced most of his work in San Francisco.

In 1889 Remington created one of his most famous illustrations, "Cowboys Coming to Town for Christmas" (Plate 16), which appeared double-page in *Harper's Weekly* for December 21. It owed its inspiration in part to Rufus Zogbaum's earlier

20

"Painting the Town Red." It was not the last time the subject was to be used. Stanley Wood's "Cowboy Fireworks" (Plate 20), done for *Harper's* in 1900, relied heavily on Remington's version.

It was almost the last of the great woodcut illustration era. Henceforth photoengraving would take over and paintings instead of drawings would be reproduced by mechanical process, robbing the printed page of crisp delineation, but contributing a more accurate interpretation of the artist's work. Richard Harding Davis, a renowned writer of the period, did an article for *Harper's* in April of 1892, entitled "West from a Car Window." Remington's illustrations (Illus. 32) for this article were reproduced in photogravure from wash drawings and gave a good indication of what the originals must have looked like. Henceforth, the artist's prolific illustration was to be reproduced in this wash medium. Not many of Remington's first drawings exist in the original, probably having been destroyed in the process of transfer to the wood block; therefore, these photogravure reproductions afford a fairly close look at his early work. Though now less frequently illustrating articles on cowboys, Remington provided a "Bucking Bronc" (Plate 18) for a large lithograph published by Davis and Sanford of New York in 1895. The same year he wrote and illustrated an article on an entirely overlooked cowboy on the American scene, the "Cracker Cowboys of Florida" (Illus. 33, 34). Here was a cowboy surely, but not the type for a romantic image; possibly Remington gave him his only exposure in the public prints.

Leslie's Weekly magazine attempted to keep up with the western surge and carried Dan Smith's "A Race on the Plains" (Plate 17) as a cover illustration in a January 1892 issue.

Charles M. Russell, while achieving his greatest fame after the turn of the century, collaborated at this time with J. H.

Illus. 33

Illus. 34

Smith, another illustrator for *Leslie's Weekly,* and in 1889 they produced a full-page composite, "Bronco Ponies and Their Uses—How They Are Trained and Broken" (Plate 19). The same year Russell illustrated for *Harper's,* but it was not until much later, beyond the scope of this book's material, that he and many others rose to prominence in the field of western illustration. A drawing in 1908 for the *American Review of Reviews* (Illus. 36) shows the style which became his trademark, a free pen and ink rendering with an excellent feeling for action. Illustration 37 shows clearly Russell's radical departure in style from previous artists.

Another artist rising on the scene was Maynard Dixon whose illustrations, while not always of cowboy subject matter, were concerned with the west. Edgar Beecher Bronson's *Cowboy Life on the Western Plains or Reminiscences of a Ranchman,* published in 1910, contained several Dixon illustrations (Illus. 35) with a crisp, fine line, and a good sense of composition. Wladyslaw T. Benda contributed a good cowboy subject to the same book (Illus. 38), though his later fame was making theatrical masks.

During the first decade of the 20th century, Frederic Remington contributed full-page illustrations to *Harper's* and *Collier's* on many subjects, among which were "The Drought in the Southwest" (Plate 21), "A Post Office in the 'Cow Country'" (Plate 22), a subject first explored by W. A. Rogers (Illus. 8) two decades earlier, "Killing a Cattle Thief" (Plate 23), and "Desperate Riding in the Cattle Country—A Pony Caught in a Gopher Hole," "Life in the Cattle Country—Driving the Round Up," "The Round Up," all difficult to reproduce from the gravure of the time, having been photoengraved from paintings.

Books and articles on the west continued to pour forth to a new audience after the turn of the century. The men who had gone west to be cowboys were long since gone or were ranchers owning large spreads and the new breed of cowboy wasn't quite the adventurous daredevil of the 1870s and '80s. Cattle thieving and shoot-ups in town were still in evidence, but not many men stretched a rope and fewer were treated to impromptu justice. Many of the artist-illustrators of the previous decades had become much sought-after painters who painted from memory those exciting adventures of their youth.

Charles Schreyvogel, an artist whose career began in the 1890s like many others, achieved his fame after the turn of the century and joined artists like H. W. Hansen whose most important work lay in the field of painting—more exactly, painting used as illustration, to which must be added the work of N. C. Wyeth who came west shortly after the turn of the century and during his lifetime painted many fine canvasses based on his first-hand experience in the southwest.

Charles Russell continued to illustrate for the magazines with his unique style of drawing, as seen in his 1910 work which accompanied George Pattullo's story of "Corazón" in *McClure's* (Plates 25, 26, 27). He also contributed to *Leslie's Weekly's* program of full-page reproduction of paintings, some in color. "Christmas Dinner for Men on the Trail" (Plate 24), done in 1905, was one of these.

* * *

Illus. 36

23

Illus. 37

24

The 20th century artists continued to illustrate the cowboy, but many conceived of him as an image separate and apart from his profession and a fitting subject for art. Those who have endlessly recreated him in this period are too numerous to mention and the amount of material too overwhelming to put between covers. Thus limited, it seemed appropriate to select the work of graphic artists who have created him in print form, as had, in effect, the illustrators of the previous era with their woodcuts.

The popularity of etching after the turn of the century made it the natural print medium and those who used it included such persons as Edward Borein and Levon West. Borein did over a hundred subjects relating to the cowboy and ranching and produced far more than anyone today on this subject. Later, lithography and woodcuts became a popular medium. Many prominent artists did not essay to create in the print medium and hence do not come within the scope of this group of reproductions. Others of the 20th century artists only approached the subject in one or two prints. Many, but not all, knew the subject first hand, such as Peter Hurd and Theodore Van Soelen. Undoubtedly there are others undiscovered here who contributed to the theme.

The subject matter of the 20th century artists—cowboys on the town, working on the ranch, taming broncs—is similar to that of their 19th century fellow artists. If any new subject matter has been added it is that of the rodeo cowboy. He evolved out of cowboy's play and he is a different breed than his older

counterpart. Often he is not at all a part of real ranching, but the public has blurred the line of distinction and his present image may well be the last vestige of a flesh and blood cowboy and will pass in time into the folklore of the genre.

Thus did efforts of the writers and artists of the second half of the 19th century build, in words and drawings, the foundations for the romantic cowboy, creating this image from the whole American cloth. They endowed him with super emotions and strengths and they passed him along to the 20th century writers and artists who keep him alive and well. They have been ably assisted by the movies and TV and the screen images of William S. Hart, Buck Jones, John Wayne, and Robert Redford, to name only a few. But they have modified his dress for the man in the street and they have given him a hundred things to glamorize from cigarettes to mouthwash.

So image and reality were crassly split. America wanted a folk hero they could believe in; the image emerged from the brushes and pens of his creators. Today his pale pickup-driving counterpart cannot hold a candle to the romance and allure of Remington's and Russell's "riders of the purple sage."

The real cowboy died long ago and Owen Wister wrote his epitaph in 1901:

> No more he rides, yon waif of might;
>
> He was the song the eagle sings;
>
> Strong as the eagle's his delight,
>
> For like his rope, his heart had wings.

JOHN MEIGS
San Patricio

NINETEENTH CENTURY

A. R. WAUD
A Drove of Texas Cattle Crossing a Stream
Harper's Weekly October 19, 1867

Plate 1

W. M. CARY
Cattle Raid on the Texas Border
Harper's Weekly January 31, 1874

30

Plate 2

FRENZENY & TAVERNIER
Calling the Night Guard
Harper's Weekly March 28, 1874

Plate 3

FRENZENY & TAVERNIER
Guarding the Herd
Harper's Weekly March 28, 1874

Plate 4

W. J. PALMER
Driving Cattle into a Corral in the Far West
Harper's Weekly September 11, 1875

W.J.Palmer Sc.

Plate 5

W. A. Rogers
Betting on the Bull-fight

Harper's Weekly November 27, 1880

Plate 6

W. A. Rogers
Breaking Camp

Harper's Weekly October 2, 1880

Plate 7

L. W. MacDonald
Cowboys Checking a Stampede of Thunder-frightened Cattle
Frank Leslie's Illustrated Weekly May 28, 1881

Plate 8

W. A. ROGERS
Roused by a Scout

Harper's Weekly February 25, 1882

Plate 9

W. A. ROGERS
Life in a Dug-out

Harper's Weekly November 18, 1882

Plate 10

W. A. ROGERS
Lassoing and Branding Calves
Harper's Weekly October 6, 1883

Plate 11

R. F. ZOGBAUM
Painting the Town Red
Harper's Weekly October 16, 1886

Plate 12

FREDERIC REMINGTON
A Quarrel Over Cards
Harper's Weekly April 23, 1887

Plate 13

FREDERIC REMINGTON
An Episode in the Opening Up of a Cattle Country
The Century Illustrated Monthly Magazine February 1888

Plate 14

FREDERIC REMINGTON
The Round-up
Century April 1888

Plate 15

FREDERIC REMINGTON
Cow-boys Coming to Town for Christmas
Harper's Weekly December 21, 1889

Plate 16

Dan Smith
The Race on the Plains
Leslie's Weekly January 9, 1892

61

Plate 17

FREDERIC REMINGTON
62   Bucking Bronc

Frederic Remington

63

Plate 18

Charles M. Russell & J. H. Smith
Bronco Ponies and Their Uses—How They Are Trained and Broken
Leslie's Weekly May 18, 1889

Plate 19

STANLEY L. WOOD
Cowboy Fireworks
Harper's Weekly 1900

Plate 20

Frederic Remington
The Drought in the Southwest
Harper's Weekly November 3, 1'00

Plate 21

Frederic Remington
A Post Office in the "Cow Country"
Collier's Weekly October 5, 1901

Plate 22

FREDERIC REMINGTON
Killing a Cattle Thief
Collier's Weekly September 7, 1901

Plate 23

CHARLES M. RUSSELL
Christmas Dinner for the Men on the Trail
Leslie's Weekly December 14, 1905

Plate 24

CHARLES M. RUSSELL
Corazon Leads His Wild Herd
McClure's Magazine July, 1910

Plate 25

CHARLES M. RUSSELL
The Steer Was Tossed Clear off the Ground
McClure's Magazine July, 1910

79

Plate 26

CHARLES M. RUSSELL
Corazón Reared Straight Up
McClure's Magazine July, 1910

81

Plate 27

THE TWENTIETH CENTURY ARTISTS

C. W. ANDERSON
born Wahoo, Nebraska 1891
now works in Mason,
New Hampshire

LAWRENCE BARRETT
born Guthrie, Oklahoma, 1897
now works in Colorado Springs,
Colorado

JOE BEELER
born Joplin, Missouri, 1931
now works in Sedona, Arizona

THOMAS HART BENTON
born Neosho, Missouri, 1889
now works in Kansas City,
Missouri

EDWARD BOREIN
born San Leandro, California,
1873
died 1945

JERRY BYWATERS
born Paris, Texas, 1906
now works in Dallas, Texas

OTIS DOZIER
born Forney, Texas, 1904
now works in Dallas, Texas

ALEXANDRE HOGUE
born Memphis, Missouri, 1898
now works in Tulsa, Oklahoma

PETER HURD
born Roswell, New Mexico, 1904
now works in San Patricio,
New Mexico

HARRY JACKSON
born Chicago, Illinois, 1924
now works in Camaiore, Italy

WALT JOHNSTON
born Washington, D. C., 1932
now works in Albuquerque,
New Mexico

GENE KLOSS
born Oakland, California, 1903
now works in Cory, Colorado

WALT KUHN
born New York, New York, 1880
died 1949

FLETCHER MARTIN
born Palisade, Colorado, 1904
now works in Roswell,
New Mexico

MERRITT MAUZEY
born Clifton, Texas, 1898
now works in Dallas, Texas

FRANK MECHAU, JR.
born Wakeeney, Kansas, 1904
died 1946

WILLIAM OBERHARDT
born Guttenberg, New Jersey,
1882
died 1958

FREDERICK O'HARA
born Ottawa, Canada, 1904
now works in Albuquerque,
New Mexico

R. H. PALENSKE
born Chicago, Illinois, 1884
died 1954

WOLFGANG POGZEBA
born Planegg, Germany, 1936
now works in Denver, Colorado

TOM RYAN
born Springfield, Illinois 1922
now works in Lubbock, Texas

GEORGES SCHREIBER
born Brussels, Belgium, 1904
now works in New York,
New York

GORDON SNIDOW
born Paris, Missouri, 1936
now works in Belen, New Mexico

JACK VAN RYDER
born Continental, Arizona, 1898
died 1968

THEODORE VAN SOELEN
born St. Paul, Minnesota, 1890
died 1964

JUSTIN WELLS
born Elk City, Oklahoma, 1941
now works in Edmond, Oklahoma

LEVON WEST
born Centerville, South Dakota,
1900
died 1968

OLAF WIEGHORST
born Viborg, Denmark, 1899
now works in El Cajon, California

HENRY ZIEGLER
born Sherman, Texas, 1889

TWENTIETH CENTURY

C. W. ANDERSON
Rodeo Sketches
84   *12" x 16" Lithograph*

Rodeo Sketches

Plate 28

LAWRENCE BARRETT
Horse Wrangler
86   8¾" x 12¼" Lithograph

Horse Wrangler   Laurence Barrett

Plate 29

Joe Beeler
An Arizona Cowboy
13" x 15" Lithograph

89

Plate 30

THOMAS HART BENTON
The Corral
90   *9½″ x 13¾″ Lithograph*

Plate 31

EDWARD BOREIN
Dividing the Riders
$6^{5}\!/_{16}''$ x $11^{3}\!/_{4}''$ Etching

Plate 32

93

EDWARD BOREIN
The Longhorns
94    $9^{13}/_{16}''$ x $7^{7}/_{16}''$ *Etching*

95

Plate 33

EDWARD BOREIN
Roundup Boss
96   9⅞" x 6⅞" Etching

97

Plate 34

EDWARD BOREIN
The Wicked Pony
9⅞″ x 7⅞″ Etching

99

Plate 35

JERRY BYWATERS
Ranch Hand and Pony
10″ x 15″ Lithograph

JERRY BYWATERS

Plate 36

OTIS DOZIER
Wild Cow Milking
102   9" x 13" Lithograph

Wild cow milking contest (Rodeo) 15 prints   Otis Dozier '40

Plate 37

ALEXANDRE HOGUE
Cap Rock Ranch
104   *7⅛″ x 12″ Lithograph*

Plate 38

ALEXANDRE HOGUE
Desert Glare
106   7" x 11⅞" Lithograph

Desert place

Plate 39

PETER HURD
El Borracho
108   15¾" x 12¼" Lithograph

109

Plate 40

PETER HURD
From the Bunkhouse
110   *12⅞″ x 9⅜″ Lithograph*

From the Bunk House 16/50

Peter Hurd

Plate 41

111

PETER HURD
Windmill Checker
11½" x 8½" Lithograph

113

Plate 42

HARRY JACKSON
Roping a Calf
4⅞" x 6⅜" *Etching*

Plate 43

115

HARRY JACKSON
Range Burial
12" x 19¾" Lithograph

Plate 44

WALT JOHNSTON
Hunkered
118   10⅜" x 10" Lithograph

34/75   1971   Plate 45

119

WALT JOHNSTON
Rain Slicker
14½″ x 8″ Lithograph

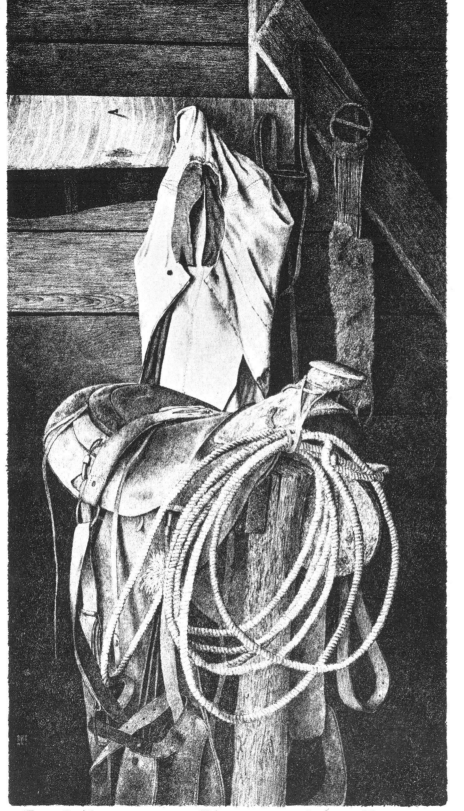

121

Rain Slicker   59/95   [signature] 1970   Plate 46

Gene Kloss
Winter Roundup
9" x 15" Etching and Aquatint

Winter Roundup Ed 35   [signature] imp

Plate 47

WALT KUHN
Christmas in the Longhorn Saloon

124

12½" x 15⅛" Lithograph

Plate 48

FLETCHER MARTIN
Rodeo
126   15" x 11½" Lithograph

127

Plate 49

MERRITT MAUZEY
Prickly Pears
128   *16½″ x 10⅜″ Lithograph*

Prickly Pears   Ed 20   Merritt Mauzey

129

Plate 50

MERRITT MAUZEY
Snubbing Post
130   11¼" x 16¾" Lithograph

"Snubbing Post"   Ed 20   Merritt Mapg

Plate 51

FRANK MECHAU
The Way Home
132   *8" x 13" Lithograph*

The Way Home

Frank Mechau '45

Plate 52

WILLIAM OBERHARDT
Cowboy
134   *13″ x 10¼″ Lithograph*

OBERHARDT

135

Plate 53

FREDERICK O'HARA
Rodeo
136   *11¾" x 30" Color Wood Cut*

Plate 54

R. H. Palenske
Over the Pass
10" x 12" Etching

"Over the Pass"

R. H. Palenske

Plate 55

WOLFGANG POGZEBA
Ready to Mount

140

9" x 11¾" Etching and Aquatint

119/150 Ready to Mount   Wolf ... /65

Plate 56

WOLFGANG POGZEBA
Roundup
9" x 11¾" Etching

Roundup 48/65   Wolf ... 58/65

Plate 57

Tom Ryan
Passing By
12" x 17" Lithograph

Plate 58

GEORGES SCHREIBER
In Texas
9¾" x 13½" Lithograph

"In Terror"

G. Schreiber

Plate 59

GEORGES SCHREIBER
Mare and Colt
148   9½″ x 13¾″ Lithograph

Plate 60

GORDON SNIDOW
Lewis
8¾″ x 7¼″ Sepia Lithograph

151

Plate 61

GORDON SNIDOW
A Cowboy's Sixth Sense
13" x 17⅜" Lithograph

Plate 62

GORDON SNIDOW
Homeward Bound
154   *13⅛″ x 17⅜″ Lithograph*

Homeward Bound 63/100

Plate 63

GORDON SNIDOW
Sandstorm
11⅛" x 13⅜" Lithograph

Plate 64

Jack Van Ryder
Picking Out His Mount
Slipping His Pack
5¼″ x 4⅛″, 5″ x 4⅜″ Etchings

Plate 65

THEODORE VAN SOELEN
Bridling the Buckskin
160   *19⅜" x 12¼" Lithograph*

66/100   Bridling the Buckskin   Van Soelen D.A.

Plate 66

THEODORE VAN SOELEN
The Cook
162   *13¾" x 19⅝" Lithograph*

VS O5L

95/100   The Cook   Van Soelen N.

Plate 67

THEODORE VAN SOELEN
Noon on the Diamond A
14" x 19" Lithograph

164

44/60   Moon on the Diamond A   Van Soelen, N.A.

Plate 68

THEODORE VAN SOELEN
Shipping

13⅞″ x 17⅞″ Lithograph

VS

$^{11}/_{15}$ © '54 Van Soelen N.A.   Shipping

Plate 69

JUSTIN WELLS
Chuckwagon
168   *11½" x 20" Woodcut*

Plate 70

Levon West
The Camp
8¾" x 14¾" Drypoint

Levon West   On Lake, Montana   January 1935   Levon West imp.

27.

Plate 71

LEVON WEST
Dust
172   9¼" x 13¾" Drypoint

Plate 72

OLAF WIEGHORST
In Trouble
174   7½" x 5¾" Etching

175

Plate 73

HENRY ZIEGLER
He Stepped into a Gopher Hole
9¾" x 7¾" *Etching*

177

Plate 74

HENRY ZIEGLER
Riding Pretty
178   6¾" x 5¾" Etching

Plate 75

179

ACKNOWLEDGMENTS

A book requiring the assembling of material from many sources usually means that there are many helping hands and minds. This book is no exception and I wish to gratefully acknowledge the people who have been of invaluable assistance in its preparation.

By a fortuitous circumstance the Women's Division of the Lubbock, Texas Chamber of Commerce approached me over a year ago about the direction their collection of prints, housed at The Museum, Texas Tech University, should take. For the two previous years I had been researching a book about the cowboy in American prints. The women of this most active group readily agreed to provide funds for the purchase of both 19th and 20th century contemporary and original prints by American artists on cowboy subjects for the collection. Since that time I have located and forwarded for their approval many prints, most of which they purchased for the collection. After its initial showing at The Museum, Texas Tech University in the Fall of 1972, the collection will be available as a traveling exhibit to museums and colleges.

Darlene Anderson, Pauline Bean, Adelaide Morganti, and Mary Nell Strong of the Women's Division have been particularly helpful, as well as Perry Gott and the director of the Lubbock Chamber of Commerce, John Logan.

James Baker, director of the Baker Gallery in Lubbock, has been invaluable from the outset in providing photographs and information and giving unstintingly of his time and that of his staff in aiding my research. Mr. Baker also arranged with Burr Miller of New York for the printing of the limited-edition lithograph.

Eugene Kingman, director of the art collections of The Museum, Texas Tech University, has provided me with full information on the prints already in their collection and technical data on the new prints as they were acquired. Other museum personnel of great assistance include: Bill Dickson, Wichita Art Association; Esther Houseman, registrar, and Berian Delabano, curator of prints, Dallas Museum of Fine Arts; C. Dean Lee, assistant curator, Fort Worth Art Center Museum; Dean Krakel, managing director, National Cowboy Hall of Fame, Oklahoma City; and Mitchell A. Wilder, Amon Carter Museum of Western Art, Fort Worth.

A special word of thanks to Sylvia Polovich of the Chicago Public Library Research Department; Paul Weaver of the Northland Press and Warren Howell of John Howell—Books in San Francisco, both of whom loaned negatives from their own publications; Charles Clegg for access to his files of *Harper's* and *Leslie's Weekly* magazines of the last century; and Phil Kovinich for research on early artists.

In addition to the prints from the permanent collection I wish to thank Mr. and Mrs. Niblick Thorne and the following artists for loan of prints or other assistance: Bill Moyer, Tom Ryan, Gordon Snidow, Olaf Wieghorst, Harry Jackson, Walt Johnston, Wolfgang Pogzeba, Jerry Bywaters, and Joe Beeler, who also allowed me to reproduce his lithograph on the dust jacket. The following galleries were most generous in the loan of prints or assistance in locating items: The Baker Gallery, Lubbock; Gallery III, Ruidoso, New Mexico; Kennedy Galleries, New York; Fort Worth Art Center Museum; Dallas Museum of Fine Arts; and Sylvan Cole, Associated American Artists, New York.

The able staff of the Swallow Press have been of great aid, especially Doretta Fuhs. Louis Matis of Artists Designers Graphic of Chicago has again provided an exciting design for my second book with the Swallow Press.

Peter Hurd, friend, confidant, and neighbor, has generously created two new lithographs for this book (one for the limited edition only) for which I am deeply grateful.

And finally, Georgia Rich ably assisted me in the tedious job of processing note and reference cards. The above might lead one to the conclusion that everyone but myself prepared this book and to some extent that is most certainly true.

INDEX OF ARTISTS AND WORKS

(Entries for 20th century works include size, media, edition and ownership.)